TOTALLY WEIRD

Spiders

Tricky words are explained on page 32.

Creepy-crawly spiders!

Are you nervous about spiders? Well, don't worry! Most of them are much happier munching on insects than nibbling on you. So get ready – you're about to enter the totally weird world of spiders!

Spider breakdown

There are many different kinds of spiders, but they all have the same basic body parts. Every spider has: a body made up of a head, thorax and abdomen; eight spindly legs; a pair of razor-sharp fangs for biting prey and fighting; and spinnerets, for spinning those spectacular silky webs.

A SPIDER FLAT ON ITS BACK

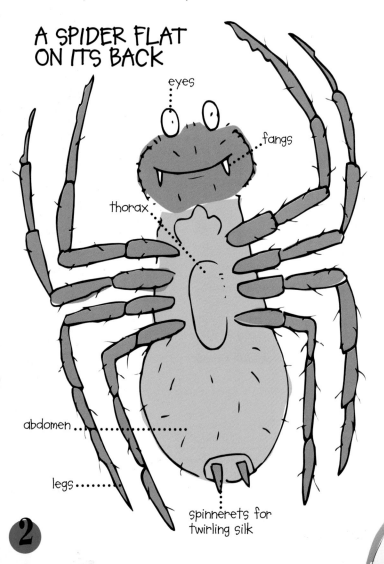

eyes

fangs

thorax

abdomen

legs

spinnerets for twirling silk

What's in a name?

Spiders belong to a bunch of animals called arachnids. Arachne was the name of a girl in an ancient Greek story who beat the goddess Athena at a weaving contest, so Athena turned her into a spider.

Just my luck!

Where in the world?

Spiders live everywhere on Earth, except Antarctica. They set up home under rocks and logs, in tunnels and trees and even underwater. Spiders have been rocketed into space to see if they can spin webs without gravity. They can!

Strange but true

Most spiders have eight eyes. Some spiders have six, four, or two eyes, and some have no eyes at all!

▲ A tiny crab spider changes its colour slowly to match the colour of the flower on which it sits. It waits patiently in ambush for a passing insect!

Home sweet home

Spiders build incredible homes, from cosy burrows to underwater bubble houses. Many spiders rig their homes with traps and trip wires to capture prey.

Cool living

How does a hairy tarantula stay cool in the sizzling desert heat? It digs a deep bunker in the sand. This underground den keeps the spider nicely chilled until the Sun goes down and the air turns cooler. Only then will it creep outside to find a bite to eat or a mate for the evening.

Hey, chill out.

It's a trap

The spider in the photograph has rigged up trigger threads around the outside of its nest. If an insect disturbs the threads, the spider will know a tasty meal is nearby.

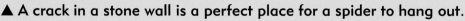
▲ A crack in a stone wall is a perfect place for a spider to hang out.

That's weird

Cave spiders are expert rock climbers. They whizz up the steep walls of their caves on their eight extra-strong, long legs.

Spider cities

Social spiders work together in construction teams to build huge spider cities. The friendly spiders link webs together to make a giant webbed sheet, big enough to cover a tree. The spiders also hunt together in groups so that they can catch and share larger prey.

UNDER CONSTRUCTION

Watery homes

A water spider builds its home underwater. First it weaves a silk platform. Then it traps an air bubble from the surface and attaches it to the platform. When the air begins to run out, the spider pops up to the surface for another bubble.

Almost home.

Knock, knock

The secretive trapdoor spider lives in a tunnel with a tightly fitting door. When visitors approach, it opens the door and gobbles them up!

▲ A trapdoor spider is a keen decorator. It waterproofs its burrow with soil. For a finishing touch, the spider adds a soft coating of spit and silk.

Waiting game

The spider spends many evenings at home, waiting patiently below its door, sometimes with its front legs just sticking out. When the spider feels the vibrations of passing prey, it rushes out, grabs and bites the prey and drags it into the burrow. Then the spider bangs the door firmly shut.

That's weird

One kind of trapdoor spider plugs the top of its burrow with its hard, flat belly, which fits snugly into the hole, just like a cork in a bottle. Now it's safe from enemies.

Would you like to come in?

Super Spinners

Spider-silk is tough, light and elastic so it's perfect for lassoing prey, making a comfortable bed, a dangerous trap or a swing to escape from danger.

Spinning silk

Spiders spin different kinds of silk for different jobs. When the spider first spins the silk, it is liquid, but it soon hardens into thread that can be stronger than steel.

Look, I'm Tarzan!

What a drag!

A spider can always make a quick getaway. Wherever a spider roams, it leaves a trail of thin silk thread, called a dragline, which works just like a swing. When the spider is threatened, it jumps on to the dragline and swings to safety.

SILK FOR KEEPING EGGS SAFE

SILK for DRAGLINES

SILK for WEBS

SILK for WRAPPING PREY

Under the microscope

This picture has been magnified many times. It shows silk being spun from tiny tubes on a spider's body.

Sticky habit

Some spiders make webs out of sticky silk. A spider doesn't get stuck in its own web because it avoids the gluey threads. It also coats its body with slippery oil so that the silk doesn't stick.

OIL

Strange but true

Spiders are good at pest control. Without spiders, the world would be overrun with insects.

▲ A spider keeps its prey hidden from other hungry mouths by wrapping it up in a ball of silk.

Web masters

No one teaches a spider how to spin a web — it just knows! Different spiders spin webs in all kinds of shapes and sizes, including ones that look like big string bags, bicycle wheels and hammocks.

In the net

A net-throwing spider knits silk threads to make a hand-held web. It doesn't sit on its web like other spiders, but holds the web in its two outstretched front legs. When an unsuspecting insect walks below, the net-throwing spider stretches the net out wide and drops it over the victim's body.

▲ A net-throwing spider's web is stretchy enough to catch and wrap up a big moth.

ORB SPIDER'S WEB

This speedy spider spins a silk bridge between two twigs...

Whee!

... then parachutes down to add supporting threads.

It spins threads from the middle to the edge, in the shape of bicycle spokes on a big wheel.

Over and under, in and out and back again.

Then the spider spins from the middle outwards. It goes round and round.

This part always makes me dizzy!

Finally, it spirals back to the middle of the web. This time, it lays one final super-sticky thread to catch its dinner.

Orb webs

Every night, most orb spiders spin a bouncy web, which contains enough thread to make a pair of silk tights. The web is light enough to blow in a breeze but extremely strong. It must be strong enough to support the spider, which is 4,000 times heavier than its web.

That's weird

A spider's web is packed with healthy nutrients. Before a spider spins a new web, it makes a yummy meal out of the old one!

Mmm, web again... delicious!

Horrible hammocks

The hammock weaver spider has a cunning plan. First, it spins a flat or slightly domed net of silk, like a hammock. Above the hammock, it sets up a mass of tangled lines. When a flying insect hits the maze of lines, it falls on to the hammock. The crafty spider is waiting, ready to gobble up the insect.

On the prowl

Many spiders are fierce warriors that go out on patrol, ready to hunt down and attack creatures that wander into their deadly paths. Others leap on to their victims and glue them to the spot with sticky spit, or even worse...

Jumping around

The jumping spider has huge eyes that swivel round like telescopes to detect movement. It creeps towards its prey, then springs up, opening its jaws in mid-flight. When it lands, it delivers a lethal bite.

Strange but true

A jumping spider can spot its prey from a long way off — over 14 times its body length!

▲ A jumping spider is a champion long-jumper. It crouches down like a cat, pushes on its back legs, then propels itself forwards.

What's in a name?

The spitting spider is named after its yucky habit of spraying prey with two streams of gruesome gluey goo. This goo makes the prey fall to the ground which gives the spider plenty of time to stroll over and kill it.

Spider burglars

A few kinds of spiders are expert thieves that steal from other spiders' webs. The burglar spider moves quietly and unseen over another spider's web, nibbling up old scraps of food. When it is really brave, it eats the main prey, too.

Soon, you'll be mine!

On your marks...

A wolf spider is a large, hairy athlete. It can look for prey in four directions at once. When it spots a tasty snack, it sprints off — with deadly accuracy.

The fishing spider spends its days dangling its front legs in ponds. When it feels the ripples made by a struggling insect that has fallen in, it grabs the unlucky creature and reels in its supper.

▼ The wandering spider is a giant of the spider world. Here it gobbles up a tree frog.

Killing machine

A tree frog's mating call means one thing to a wandering spider. The spider feels the sound vibrations and knows that dinner is on the way!

A BUG WITH BITE

Strange but true

This huge South American wandering spider measures nearly 15 cm across. That's bigger than your hand!

Night and day

A wandering spider has a hectic night-life. It hunts for frogs, lizards and insects. During the day, it has a well-deserved snooze. The weary spider spreads out on a leaf. Predators don't see it because it is well camouflaged.

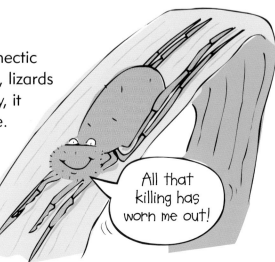

All that killing has worn me out!

Eyes front

Different types of wandering spiders have different arrangements of eyes, but they all have eight. In some types, the rows of eyes curve forwards on the head, but in others they curve backwards. Either way makes for perfect vision!

Fangs and food

Spiders are experts in the art of poisoning. A spider releases venom through fangs that look like curved claws at the end of its jaws.

Works every time!

Portia spider

The Portia spider is a crafty cannibal. It creeps into another spider's web and tugs on the silk. The web spider crawls towards the intruder thinking it has sneakily trapped an insect. Suddenly, the Portia spider attacks and eats the surprised web spider.

DINNER-TIME!

A spider stuns or kills an insect with venom from its needle-sharp fangs.

fangs

Then it spits a cocktail of juices over the insect to turn it to pulp.

Finally, the spider sucks the juicy insides out of the insect, leaving just its hard, crunchy casing.

Believe it or not

When prey is hard to find, spiders may survive for up to one year without eating.

▲ The venom that shoots through a spider's fangs is far more poisonous than snake venom.

Tell me why

SPIDERS ARE FUSSY ABOUT THEIR FOOD

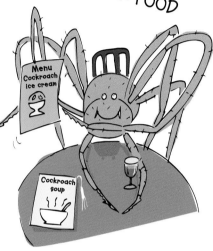

A banana spider's favourite food isn't bananas, it's the cockroaches that live on bananas! The banana spider eats little else, so people use it to help keep down the cockroach population.

This night-time hunting spider just loves woodlice. The spider pierces the woodlouse's tough exoskeleton with its enormously long fangs, so that it can get at the tasty body inside.

Danger!
Deadly spiders

Many spiders are poisonous. But don't worry, most spider bites won't harm you. There are, however, a few nasty, dangerous biters...

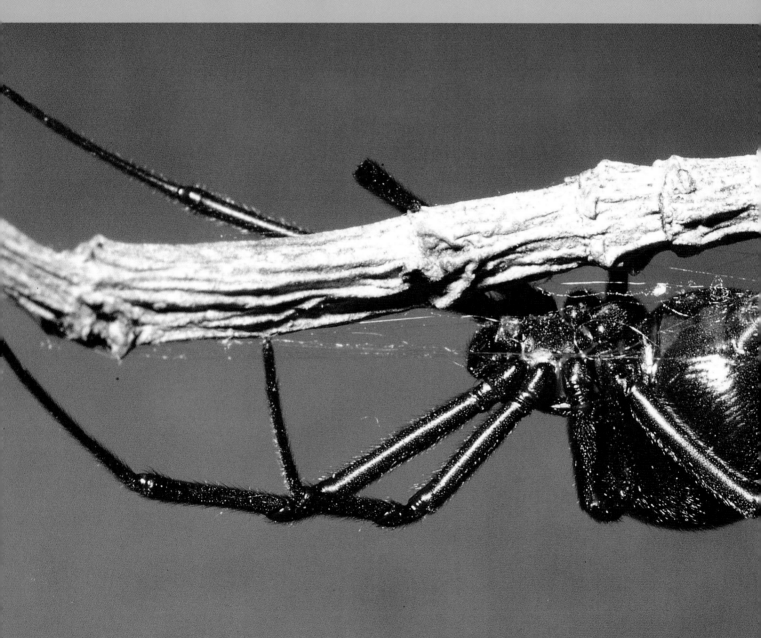

▲ The female black widow spider is about the size of an adult's thumbnail and is highly poisonous.

Strange but true

Around the world, black widow spiders have different names, including hourglass spiders and shoe-button spiders!

Black widows

The black widow spider is a shy and retiring creature. It only bites when it feels its life is threatened – it would rather run away. But accidents happen because it often finds shelter in shoes and clothes. One small bite is enough to kill.

Danger down under

The Australian funnel web spider wanders around back gardens in search of dinner. When it is disturbed, it attacks and delivers a harmful bite that's strong enough to pierce your fingernail. Victims may even die!

That's weird

The deadly violin spider has a mark on its body that looks like a violin. Usually, its bite isn't fatal, but the wound can take a long time to heal and may leave a large scar.

Hairy knees

Imagine finding a big, hairy spider like this in your bath! But don't be scared, it wouldn't harm you.

Strange but true

In some parts of the world, hairy spiders are a popular item on the menu. Have them raw or cooked, but always without the fangs!

▲ This bird-eating spider from Mexico has poor eyesight, but uses its legs to find and capture prey.

Terrifying tarantula

Do you think big spiders are scary? In the past, people believed that the bites of large European tarantulas were responsible for many deaths. In fact, the wrong spider was blamed. The real culprit turned out to be a smaller spider – the black widow. Be warned – don't judge a spider by its size.

That's weird

In Italy, when people thought they had been bitten by a tarantula, they performed a lively dance called the tarantella, to dance the poison out of their bodies.

On the defensive

Spiders are always on the look-out for prey but predators have got their eyes on spiders, too! Clever disguises and quick getaways help keep spiders alive.

Spider spears

Many big, hairy spiders shoot clouds of hairs into the faces of predators. The tiny hairs are sharp with hooked ends. They cause so much irritation that the spider has plenty of time to scuttle away from its enemy.

Rotten disguise

Some spiders avoid dangerous predators by disguising themselves as bird droppings. One kind of bird-dropping spider even spins specks of white silk around itself on a leaf. This makes it look like a fresh dropping.

Spot me if you can!

Good disguise

Many spiders keep safe by looking exactly like leaves. The spiders are mottled to match bark or mouldy leaves, green to match living leaves, or even have brown, crinkled outlines to look like dead leaves!

22

Alien bug

If you were a hungry predator, would you eat something that looked like a spaceship? The buffalo spider has a flat body, spiky spines and bright colours. Would-be predators can't work out what they've come across.

Strange but true

A spider from Madagascar disguises itself by hiding on a twig. It looks just like a dried-up bud.

That's weird

A South American tree-dwelling spider leaves its enemies all wet. It simply raises its bottom towards its attacker and squirts liquid in its face. Yuck!

A date with danger

When courting, the first thing a male spider does is to persuade the female spider not to eat him!

Strange but true

To escape the grip of a fierce female, a male spider may even leave behind some of his legs.

▲This rather anxious male spider is more than three times smaller than the female!

That's weird

A few male and female spiders enjoy a friendly get together. One will gently tug on another's web to let it know it wants to meet. Then they play 'pat-a-cake' with each other's legs.

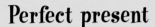

Perfect present

One type of wolf spider knows that the way to reach a female spider's heart is through her stomach! He gives his mate a grisly gift of wrapped fly. While the female guzzles up the fly, the male mates with her. He knows that as long as she is busy munching, she won't eat him!

I think she likes me.

Making a tricky move

Many kinds of male spiders wave their long, hairy legs at female spiders to show they want to be friends, rather than food! Some of these signals can be complicated. With eight legs, a spider can invent lots of natty new dance moves for that special date!

One kind of water spider announces he's on his way to a female by sending drum beats across the water. Then he pulls on her dragline, rowing himself across the water to meet her. They have a romantic chat by tapping each other's legs.

One kind of fishing spider finds an area of pond where a female spider has set up house. The male finds the female by following the fragrant scent she leaves on the water.

Growing up...
...leaving home

Some female spiders take great care of their eggs, wrapping them in a bubble of silk called an egg sac.

▲ A female wandering spider looks after her egg sac. Many other spiders abandon their eggs.

A good start

Eggs hatch into spiderlings. Burrowing spiderlings are doted on by their mother, who takes care of their every need. But lots of other spiderlings have to fend for themselves. When food is short and they are hungry, they even eat each other!

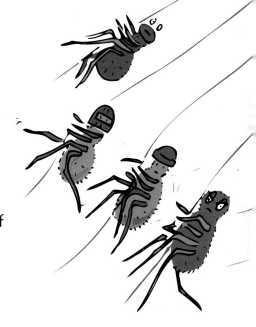

High flyers

Some spiders take to the skies, especially young spiderlings that travel long distances to find a home of their own. They rise up to dizzy heights of 1,525 metres, flying on silken threads that catch the breeze! This is called 'ballooning'.

Believe it or not

Female spiders usually live longer than males. A female trapdoor spider may live for as long as 20 years.

A SPLITTING TIME

Every time a spider gets too big for its skin, it just grows a brand-new one.

"Oh no! I'm splitting up!"

First a split appears across the spider's back. The split grows and grows.

"Phew!"

Soon the spider wriggles free of its old skin. This is called moulting.

The spider hangs around a bit for the new skin to dry. It flexes its legs in anticipation of its new look!

"I just love my new skin!"

Spider stories

Around the world, there are hundreds of stories about spiders, from hairy monster spider tales to myths about spiders as the origins of life on Earth.

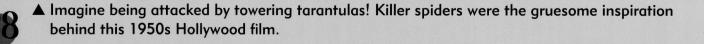

MONSTER SPIDER...CRAWLING TERROR 100 FEE

TARANTU

▲ Imagine being attacked by towering tarantulas! Killer spiders were the gruesome inspiration behind this 1950s Hollywood film.

Spider-Man

A spider has special grip pads on its feet which give it the ability to walk up walls and march across ceilings. This amazing feat was the inspiration behind the cartoon character Spider-Man. He can 'weave a web as strong as steel' to catch his enemies, too.

RESEARCHERS SEEKING CLUE!

CAN ANYTHING ESCAPE IT?

He'll never find me here.

Ceiling Thomas

In West Africa, the rascally hero of many stories is half-man, half-spider. He's called Anansi. When things are going his way, Anansi is a man, but when he's in trouble, he skilfully turns into a spider and hides on the ceiling. This trickery earned him the nickname of Ceiling Thomas.

That's weird

'Little Miss Muffet who sat on a tuffet' was a real person. Her father was a spider expert who insisted she ate mashed spiders. Until 200 years ago, this was thought to be a cure for the common cold.

Bad guys
and good guys

There are over 30,000 kinds of spiders crawling about. Some people hate them, others keep them as pets. So, are spiders good guys or bad guys? Here are more amazing facts to help you decide...

It's a set-up!

Most spiders, like this wolf spider, are harmless, but they're often blamed for other bugs' bites. The real culprits are usually blood-thirsty ticks or fleas, too small to see. The bugs quickly depart, leaving a nearby spider to be blamed for a crime it didn't commit.

Wonder webs

Spider webs could help to save people's lives. The Defense Department of the USA is attempting to use stretchy spider silk to make bullet-proof vests. The steel-like threads are strong enough to absorb the power of a flying bullet. Wow whizz!

In New Guinea, there are giant wood spiders that spin webs two metres wide. The huge, sticky traps are so tough that the people who live there use them as fishing nets!

Mean machine

A Brazilian wandering spider must be the meanest spider on Earth. It hides away in people's homes and it won't think twice about giving a fatal bite. You can't even scare it away. If you hit the fearless fiend, it will try even harder to bite!

Holy spiders

Many people believe spiders have special powers. In Polynesia, it's said that you reach heaven by climbing a giant ladder of spider silk that stretches up into the sky.

Spiders save the world

Would you like to share your home with this leggy visitor? A house spider, like most spiders, is harmless and does a great job of killing flies and other insects that spread disease. Each year, spiders eat thousands of tonnes of dangerous bugs. Yuck!

Index

Author: Christine Morley
Consultant: Jonathan Elphick
Illustrations: Phillip Morrison
Photographs: Front Cover: Natural History Photographic Agency; p3: Bruce Coleman Ltd; p4/5: Science Photo Library; p6/7: BBC Natural History Unit Picture Library; p8: Science Photo Library; p9: Planet Earth Pictures; p10: Planet Earth Pictures; p12/13: Oxford Scientific Films; p14/15: Premaphotos Wildlife; p16/17: Planet Earth Pictures; p18/19: Planet Earth Pictures; p20/21: Science Photo Library; p22: Science Photo Library; p23: Bruce Coleman Ltd; p24: BBC Natural History Unit Picture Library/Premaphotos Wildlife; p26: Premaphotos Wildlife; p27: Planet Earth Pictures; p28: The Kobal Collection/Universal; p29: Spider-Man: TM & © 1998 Marvel Characters, Inc. All Rights Reserved; p30: Natural History Photographic Agency; p31: Planet Earth Pictures.

Published by Two-Can Publishing, a division of Zenith Entertainment plc, 43-45 Dorset Street, London W1H 4AB

Created by Two-Can Design Ltd, 346 Old Street, London EC1V 9RB

ISBN: 1-85434-796-9
Dewey Decimal Classification 595.4
A catalogue record for this book is available from the British Library.

Paperback 10 9 8 7 6 5 4 3 2

Printed in Hong Kong by Wing King Tong